AF454097

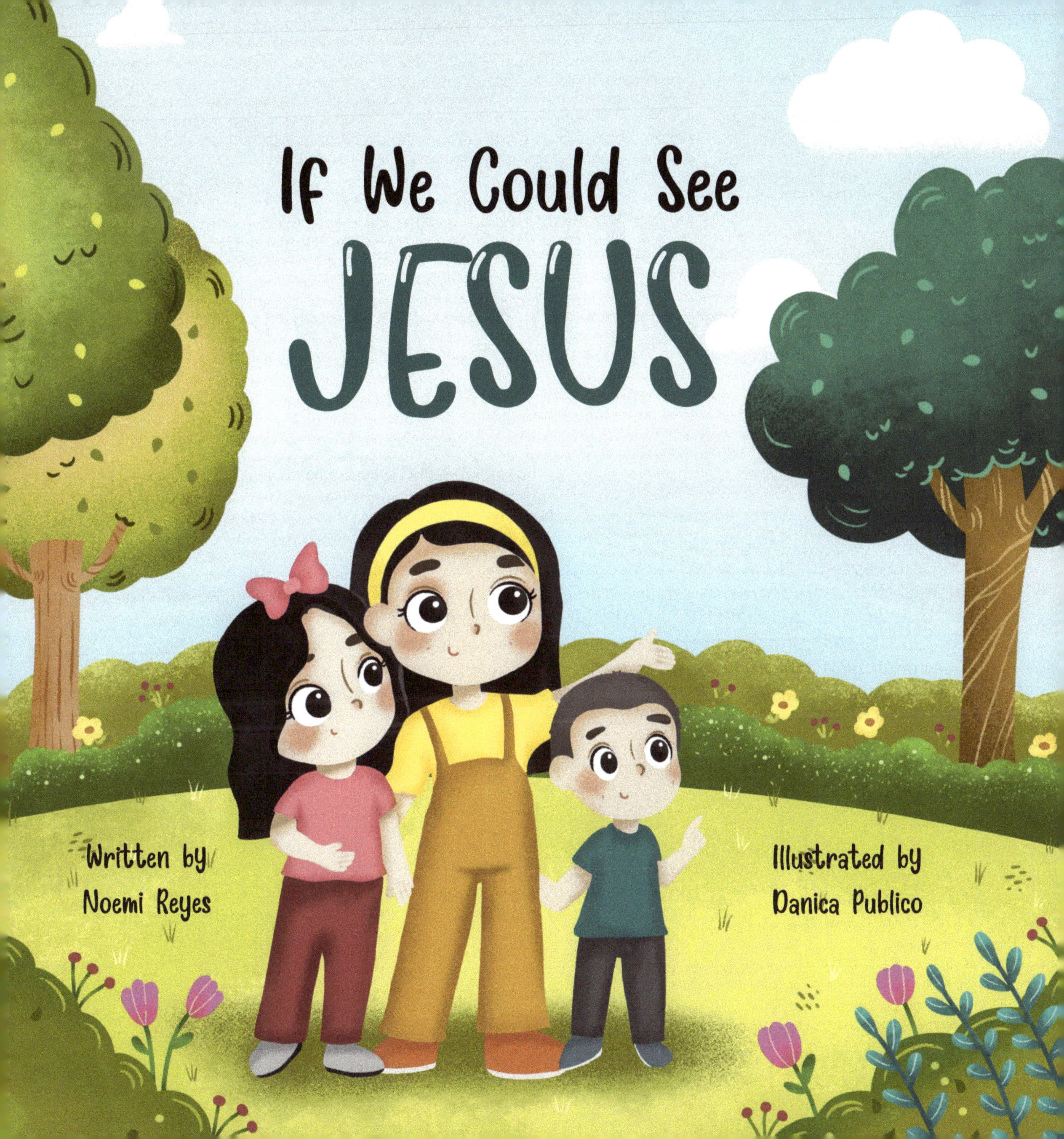

If We Could See
JESUS
Written by
Noemi Reyes
Illustrated by
Danica Publico

To my three little ones, remember that I love you and that God is always with you.

ISBN: 978-0-000000-0 (Paperback)
ISBN: 978-0-000000-0 (Hardcover)

Any references to historical events, real people, or real places are used fictitiously. Names, characters, and places are products of the author's imagination.
Written by Noemi Reyes and Illustrated by Danica Publico
First printing edition 2022

"If we could see Jesus,
would He be watching the clouds?"

"I think maybe Jesus would like something loud!"

"If I could see Jesus, we'd go horseback riding!"

"With big cowboy hats and
lasso knot tying!"

"Yes Rosie is right!"
"But if I could see Jesus I would think a circus is more fun wouldn't you say?"

"He would be the ringmaster and be center stage!"
"The lions would purr, the elephants dance, oh and don't
forget the silk acrobats!"

"If I could see Jesus I'd invite Him to skate!" "The Tic-Tac, 180, and all the best Ollies."

"Skaters in awe who then begin shouting!"
"JESUS, JESUS PLEASE SHOW US YOUR WAYS!"
"Jesus the greatest to ever skate!"

"If I could see Jesus, He'd prefer slides."
"Waterpark ones that are oh so high! The largest
ten giraffes tall and two houses wide!"

"Well if I could see Jesus He'd say scuba diving!"
"And on big huge whales, we would go riding!"

"If I could see Jesus, football games
would surely be His thing!"
"Foam fingers and nachos, a slushy or three!"
#1

"Something more classy for the King of all Kings!"
"If I could see Jesus, tea parties would be His thing!"

"We'd wear funny
hats and pearls of
all kinds!"

"And sip on some
tea while eating
small pies!"

What a delightful
afternoon
wouldn't you say
best friend?

"Seems nice I think but skydiving would be thrilling!"
"No need for a parachute because
an Angel would be willing!"

"No a safari!"
"Or maybe go camping!"

"Balloon ride!"
"Race a sports car and become the new champion!"
#1

"You guys!"

" I'm sure those are all things Jesus would love."
"But let's remember the truth in having this fun."

"Jesus, although we don't see Him right now, enjoys
the blue skies as well as the clouds."

"He's gentle and kind and loves us so much. Watching
the clouds is just what He wants."